In the Desert

Howard Rice

Table of Contents

Gambel's Quail

Jackrabbit

Rattlesnake

Where Are You?

Look around. The sky is big and blue. The ground is dry and bare. Hills of sand cross the land as far as you can see. In the distance, a string of camels walks slowly past the rising sun. It is hot and getting hotter.

Where are you?

You are in a desert, of course!

What Is a Desert?

A desert is an area of land with very little rain and, most of the time, high temperatures during the day.

In a desert, there is less than ten inches of rain each year. The ground is usually dry.

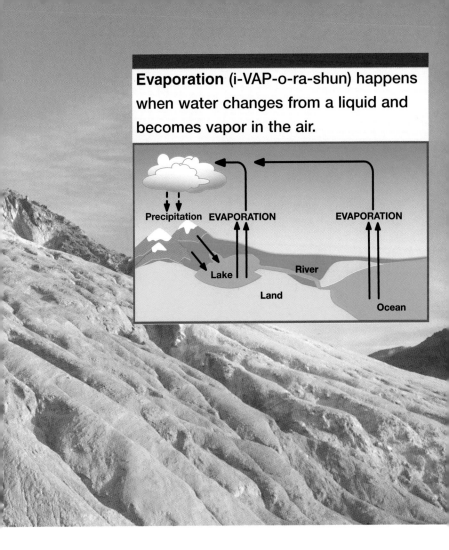

Evaporation (i-VAP-o-ra-shun) happens when water changes from a liquid and becomes vapor in the air.

Precipitation EVAPORATION EVAPORATION

Lake River

Land

Ocean

Whenever it does rain in a desert, the heat of the sun dries up most of the water again. This is called **evaporation**.

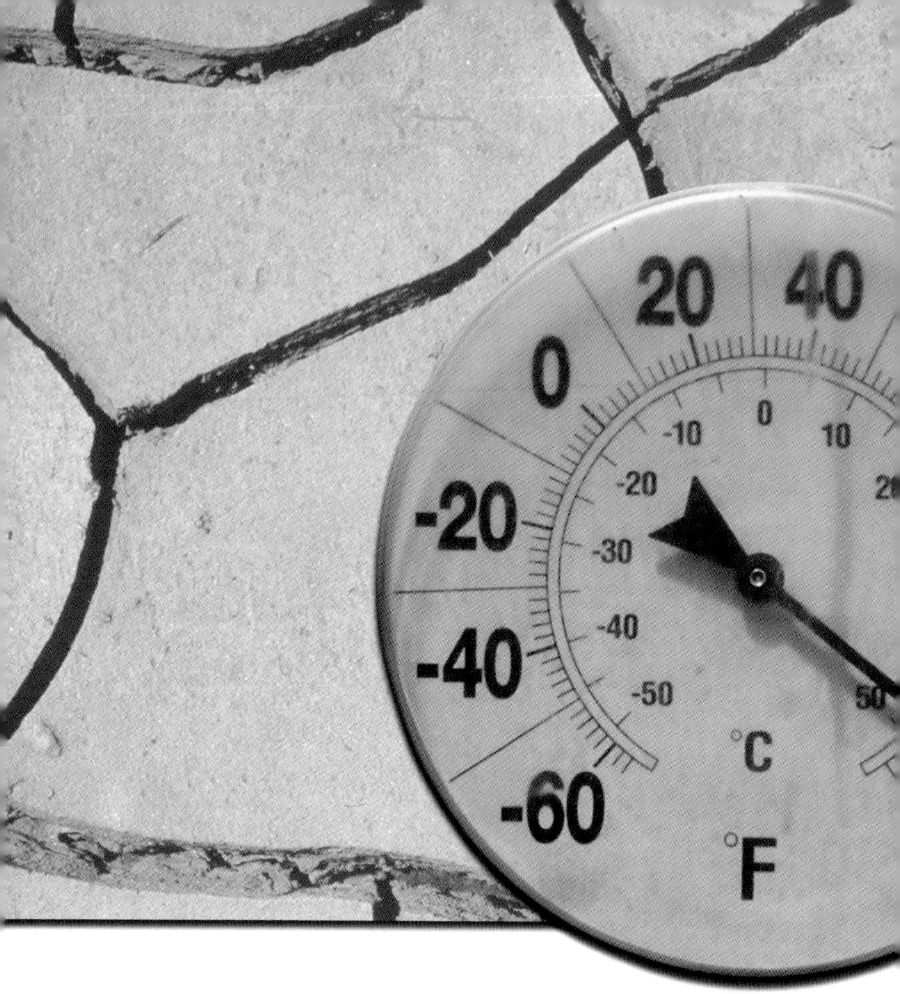
20
40
0
-10
0
10
-20
-20
-30
-40
-40
-50
-60
°C
°F

One reason for evaporation is the high temperatures. Desert nights can be cold, because during the night the ground releases its heat. But during the day, the ground soaks up the heat. The temperature

in the desert can reach as high as 130°F!

How hot is that? Most people are comfortable at about 70°F. Deserts can get almost twice that hot!

Where Are They?

Most of the deserts are in two areas called the Tropic of Cancer and the Tropic of Capricorn. Look at the map to find the tropics. The map also shows where you can find the world's great deserts.

Tropic of Cancer

The Equator

Tropic of Capricorn

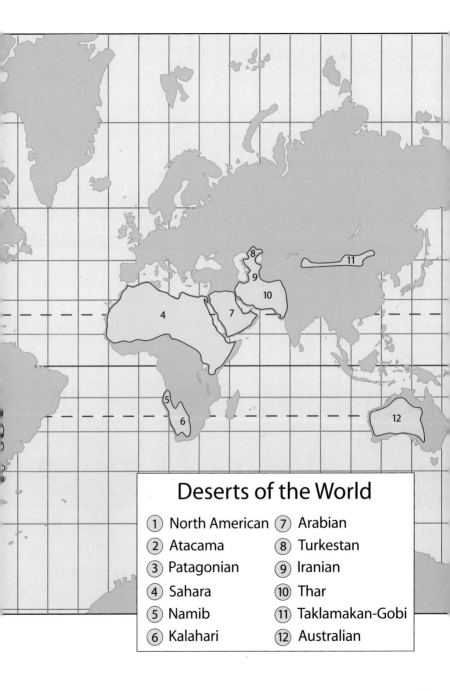

Deserts of the World

1. North American
2. Atacama
3. Patagonian
4. Sahara
5. Namib
6. Kalahari
7. Arabian
8. Turkestan
9. Iranian
10. Thar
11. Taklamakan-Gobi
12. Australian

Desert heat sometimes makes people think they see an **oasis** (o-A-sis) that is not really there.

The largest desert in the world is the Sahara. It is in Africa. Most of the Sahara gets no rain, but there are many underground rivers. Water

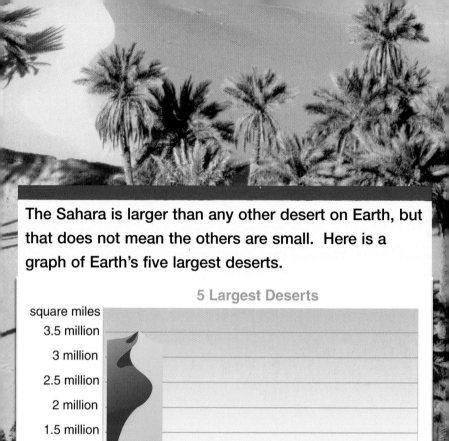

The Sahara is larger than any other desert on Earth, but that does not mean the others are small. Here is a graph of Earth's five largest deserts.

5 Largest Deserts

square miles

3.5 million	
3 million	
2.5 million	
2 million	
1.5 million	
1 million	
.5 million	
0 million	

Sahara   Arabian   Australian   Gobi   Kalahari

sometimes rises to the land. Then an **oasis** is formed. An oasis is a wet and green area in the middle of a desert.

How Are They Formed?

Many deserts are formed because of mountains. High mountains keep wetness from getting past them. Rain and snow fall on the mountains, but the air is dry by the time it gets to the desert.

Some deserts are formed because the land is far away from bodies of water. The air soaks up water from lakes and oceans, but then it rains long before it gets to the desert. The rain can not make it that far.

Even though there is not much
of it, water changes the shape of
deserts. So does wind.

You can try an **erosion** (e-RO-zhun) experiment. Make a small hill out of sand. Pour water from a pitcher down the side of the hill. What happens? Erosion!

Water and wind cause desert **erosion**. Since the land is so dry, it wears away when water or wind comes. That is what erosion means.

Strong desert wind blasts rocks and changes them, too. It also blasts sand and forms dunes. **Dunes** are like little hills spread across the desert.

When the wind comes from one direction, the **dune** (doon) is shaped like a moon. When the wind comes from many directions, the dune looks more like a star.

Can Anything Live There?

Desert Beetle

Even though there is little water, there is plant and animal life in many deserts.

Cactus Flower

The seeds of desert plants may
wait a long time underground. Once
there is rain, they grow and bloom
quickly. Other plants have long,
deep roots that reach far below the
ground for water.

21

Roadrunner

Animals in the desert have found ways to live with little water. Some sleep during the dry season. Some are able to live without water for a long time. Many sleep during the day and come out at night when it is cooler. Some even reuse the water that is already inside of them!

Coyote

Kangaroo Rat

Desert life is not for everyone. The heat and lack of water make it difficult. But as these plants and animals show, it can be done!

Glossary

desert   area of land with very little rain and usually high temperatures

dune   hill of sand formed by the wind

erosion   wearing away of land caused by water

evaporation   the changing of water from liquid into vapor

oasis   area of land in a desert with plenty of water and many growing plants

Sahara   the largest desert in the world

vapor   the gas form of a liquid